The Aztecs

Judith Crosher

Macdonald Educational

The Aztecs

The Aztecs arrived on the shores of Lake Texcoco in the Valley of Mexico in AD 1345. They were a small tribe of hunters and farmers who had wandered from the north in search of land.

Gradually, through their skill in war and their ability to learn from the people around them, they became rich and powerful. In less than two hundred years they were masters of an empire stretching from coast to coast. Fifteen million people paid them tribute every year. Their capital, Tenochtitlan, was bigger than any city in Europe. Great temples were built to honour the gods, and the fertile waters of the lake provided abundant food for the people of the city. Astronomy and the arts flourished and Aztec craftsmen produced beautiful objects of feathers, gold and precious stones.

Yet in a single year their empire was destroyed, their city razed to the ground and their people enslaved by six hundred Spaniards searching for gold.

Although the Spaniards did their best to stamp out all traces of what they thought was a bloodthirsty and pagan way of life, we still know a great deal about the Aztecs. Bernal Diaz, a Spanish officer, kept a diary describing everything he saw and did in Tenochtitlan.

After the conquest Spanish priests, sent to convert the Aztecs to Christianity, became interested in their way of life. They encouraged Aztec artists to paint pictures of their daily life. They questioned people and wrote down everything they found out about the old ways. The text and illustrations in this book are all based on these records. Together they give a picture of how ordinary people and nobles lived, worked and thought during the great days of the Aztec empire.

Contents

8 The city in the lake

10 Journey to Cactus Rock

12 People of the city

14 Trade and barter

16 Inside a house

18 Aztec cooking

20 Floating gardens

22 Educating children

24 Wives and mothers

26 Clothes and appearance

28 Sacred games

30 Learning to be a priest

32 Watching the stars

34 Offerings to the gods

36 Temples and shrines

38 Arts and crafts

40 The young warrior

42 The Aztec conquerors

44 Montezuma's empire

46 Montezuma the king

48 Defeat and conquest

50 Prices, weights and measures

51 The gods

52 Aztec writing

54 Story of the Aztecs

56 The world in the sixteenth century

58 World history AD 1100 to 1500

60 Glossary

61 Index

The main square was the centre of city life. Nine times during the day the conch shells boomed out from the temple platform, marking the divisions of the day. Every four days a market was held here, and every twenty days the people gathered to sing, dance and offer sacrifices to the gods at one of their many festivals.

A constant stream of tribesmen, bringing tribute from every corner of the empire, threaded its way across the square to the palace. Inside, the king settled the business of the empire with his council of four chiefs. In another room, Snake Woman presided over the High Court of Justice and attended to the everyday affairs of the city.

The great square in Tenochtitlan was the centre of all city life. Every month, the Aztecs celebrated the festival of one of their gods.

Processions of nobles, warriors and women dressed in gaily-coloured costumes made their way across the square towards the temple steps. The priests, with their long matted hair and black body paint, prepared for the ceremonies.

The city in the lake

A reconstructed model of the main square in Tenochtitlan

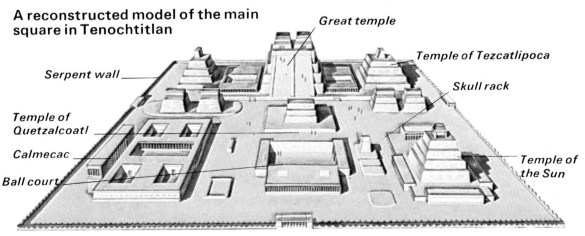

Serpent wall

Temple of Quetzalcoatl

Calmecac

Ball court

Great temple

Temple of Tezcatlipoca

Skull rack

Temple of the Sun

Journey to Cactus Rock

In about AD 1000 the Toltec empire in the Valley of Mexico was destroyed. Wandering tribes of hunters came from the north to take up free land in the valley. The last tribe to arrive was the Tenochca tribe, whom we call Aztecs.

In 1345 the Aztecs settled on the only free land left, a small island in Lake Texcoco. They lived on frogs and fish, bartering them with lakeside tribes for wood. They had to pay tribute to the powerful Tepanec tribe until, with three other tribes, they defeated the Tepanecs and gradually conquered the whole valley.

With the tribute other tribes now had to pay them, the Aztecs built Tenochtitlan. Toltec craftsmen settled in the city and taught the Aztecs many of their valuable skills. Through war, the Aztecs became richer and more powerful until in 1519 they controlled a large empire.

▲ This photograph shows the canals near Mexico City today. The Aztecs built their capital, Tenochtitlan, on Lake Texcoco, cutting canals through the swampy lake. They had very few roads and used the canals as main thoroughfares.

► The Aztec histories say that they once lived on the island of Aztlan. In a cave on the shore they found a statue of the god Blue Hummingbird, who told them to travel to a new land. The picture above shows the four tribal chiefs setting out on the journey. The artist has put the symbol for each tribe above the chiefs.

▼ The Aztecs had no wheeled transport. They carried all heavy goods in flat-bottomed boats.

► This picture shows the end of the Aztecs' quest. Their chiefs find the sign promised by the god, an eagle sitting on a cactus on a rock. This was where they had to build their city. They called it Tenochtitlan, which means *cactus rock*. The blue lines represent the waters of the lake.

The Valley of Mexico is 2000 metres above sea level and is surrounded by ranges of volcanic mountains. When the Aztecs reached the valley there were five lakes joined together. Lake Texcoco was swampy and only four metres deep. Today, Mexico City stands on the ruins of ancient Tenochtitlan.

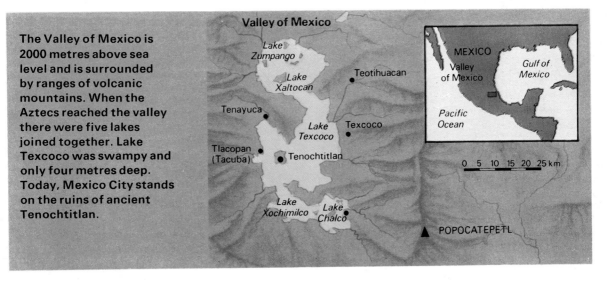

Valley of Mexico

Lake Zumpango
Lake Xaltocan
Teotihuacan
Tenayuca
Lake Texcoco
Texcoco
Tlacopan (Tacuba)
Tenochtitlan
Lake Xochimilco
Lake Chalco
POPOCATEPETL

MEXICO
Valley of Mexico
Gulf of Mexico
Pacific Ocean

0 5 10 15 20 25 km

People of the city

The king and Snake Woman shared the government of the state. The king was responsible for foreign affairs and war, while Snake Woman controlled the city's laws, taxes, food and building. There was also a council of chief officials who advised the king and Snake Woman, and who elected each king.

The only way to join the nobility was by bravery in war, as this was what the Aztecs most admired. The king chose the best warriors to be officials and gave them land, cloaks and jewellery. Clothes showed how well each person had served the state; if anyone dressed above his rank he could be punished by death. Both nobles' and peasants' sons had to earn their promotion through bravery in war.

Within the city there were several clans. Each clan lived in its own district around its temple and school. The clan owned all the land in its district and gave men plots to farm when they married. Men who did not belong to a clan had to work on nobles' farms. The clans each had a council which judged minor crimes, collected government taxes and organized members to dig canals.

▲ The king, wearing his turquoise crown, distributes goods to his people. Many of these goods have come from conquered cities. Once a year, and in times of famine, the king gave food and cloaks to the poor of the city.

◄ Four officials are passing judgement on two prisoners. Nobles were punished more severely than ordinary people. Thieves had to repay twice what they had stolen. Crop stealers and drunken nobles were put to death outside the court. There was no prison.

Slaves were either prisoners of war, criminals or poor people who had sold themselves into slavery. Ordinary people were given their own land to farm by the clan, while peasants without land worked on nobles' farms.

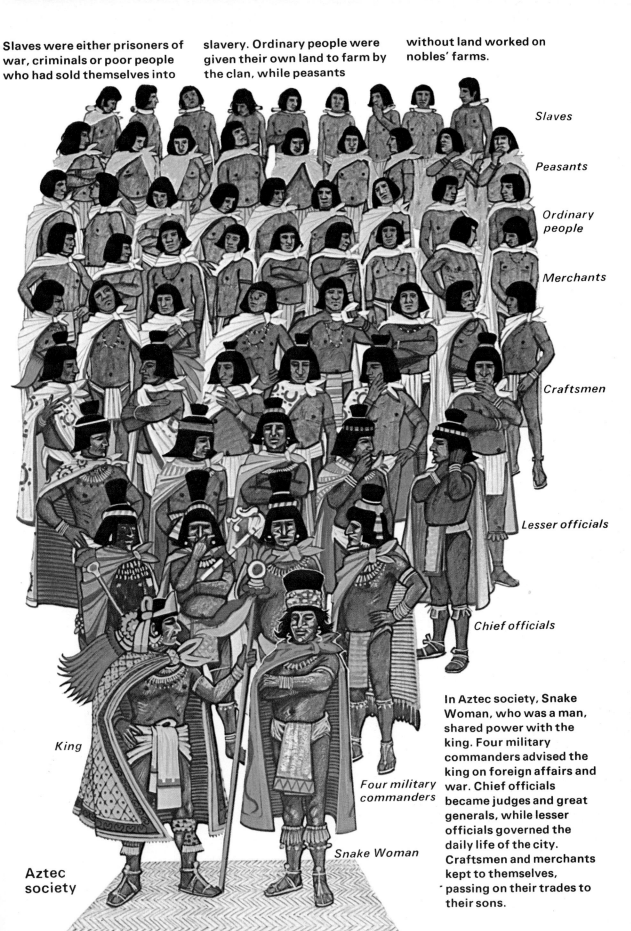

Slaves

Peasants

Ordinary people

Merchants

Craftsmen

Lesser officials

Chief officials

King

Four military commanders

Snake Woman

Aztec society

In Aztec society, Snake Woman, who was a man, shared power with the king. Four military commanders advised the king on foreign affairs and war. Chief officials became judges and great generals, while lesser officials governed the daily life of the city. Craftsmen and merchants kept to themselves, passing on their trades to their sons.

Trade and barter

When the Spanish soldier, Bernal Diaz, saw the market of Tlatelolco he wrote this description in his journal; "Our soldiers, who had been in Constantinople, in Rome and all over Italy said that they had never seen a market so well laid out, so orderly and so full of people."

Every trader paid a fee to the market supervisor. His officials mingled with the crowd, smashing false measures and confiscating the whole stock of anyone found selling shoddy goods. A court sat at one end of the market. Anyone caught stealing was tried immediately and, if found guilty, was beaten to death then and there.

▼ This painting of the market place by the modern Mexican artist, Hernandez, is based on Aztec pictures. It shows the enormous variety of goods which could always be bought.

More than 60,000 people came to the market every day. There was no money, so people bartered, using cocoa beans as small change. Farmers' wives sat behind heaps of vegetables on rush mats. Hill tribesmen brought goose quills full of gold dust. There were potters and copper axe sellers, feather merchants and jewellers, women selling hot tortillas, and healers with herbs and potions. Naked Huaxtecs brought fattened puppies to be sold as a delicacy for the Aztec table.

In the slave section there were prisoners of war, criminals or men made penniless by gambling who had come to sell themselves. Slaves would sometimes try to escape at the moment of purchase. If they could reach the king's palace without being caught, they were free. Only their buyer was allowed to chase them.

▲ A wooden collar around his neck meant that a slave was being sold because he was lazy or a thief. Sometimes, poor families became slaves to avoid starvation.

▼ In the middle of the one-roomed thatched peasants' hut burned the smoky fire around which the family ate and slept. Rush sleeping mats, woven by the women, covered the earth floor and a blanket was used to cover the doorway. A pottery figure of the god of the family stood in a niche in the wall.

Inside a house

Peasants built their huts around the edge of the city. They kept turkeys and rabbits, which scratched in the garden between the beehive and grainbin for food. Craftsmen lived nearer the centre in mud-brick houses, built so that each room led on to a central courtyard. The nobles' palaces, built of whitewashed stone and with over a hundred rooms, were around the main plaza. The patios and flat roofs were covered with flower gardens.

Inside the houses, the rooms were almost bare. Mats lay on the floors, as everyone from king to slave slept on a mat on the floor. Light came from wooden torches on the wall and round the room were stored the family's possessions and objects of daily use. There were the husband's digging stick and fishing nets, the wife's loom, the cooking and storage pots and baskets. Even palaces had no doors, but the doorways were hung with cloths sewn with copper bells, allowing cool air to circulate through the house.

▲ Most families had a mud brick bath-house in the garden. They lit a fire against the back wall, then crawled in. They threw water on the red hot wall to make steam, and beat themselves with a bundle of twigs to clean their skin. The steam bath was also used to cure illnesses.

Aztec cooking

Poor people

Peasants lived mainly on maize and beans, apart from a duck or a crow they might trap in the garden. Their only domestic animals were rabbits, dogs and turkeys, which were saved and fattened for special occasions. Maize was the staple food of the Aztecs. Every morning the women ground it into flour and boiled it into a porridge, which they flavoured with sage. Otherwise there were steamed pancakes stuffed with tadpoles, cactus worms or fish. Another favourite was tortillas, grilled and dipped in a tomato and hot pepper stew.

Richer people enjoyed turtles and crabs imported from the coast. It is said that King Montezuma chose from a hundred different dishes every day, including wild pig and pheasant from the hills. Even the king ate with his fingers, but it was polite to wash one's hands and face before and after eating.

▲ The Spaniards were shocked by the Aztecs' favourite food, roast puppy. Every family kept some of these hairless dogs to eat on special occasions.

▲ Tortillas were made fresh every day. The maize was first ground into flour. The women mixed the flour with water and moulded the dough into flat pancakes. These were grilled on a flat dry stone over the fire.

◄ When the Aztecs first came to Tenochtitlan, the only food they could find was from the marshy lake. They netted water birds and caught frogs, newts, water-fly eggs and fish. They continued to use these foods as they were only allowed to hunt other game once a year.

▼ Nobles' parties lasted all night. Guests came in litters with gifts of flowers. After dinner they smoked clay pipes filled with tobacco and drank cocoa frothed with vanilla. They were entertained with music and juggling acts.

Floating gardens

▲ Tenochtitlan, which means *Cactus Rock*, was built on a tiny island in a shallow lake. Instead of roads, the people used canals for transport and used mud to enlarge the island. Only the ground at the centre of the island could support stone houses. Three stone causeways ran to the mainland and an aqueduct brought fresh water to the city.

◀ The farmer's main tool was a wooden digging stick. He planted his seeds in groups of five: one at each corner for the four winds and one in the centre for the god of growth.

Agave cactus

▲ The agave cactus grew wild. The Aztecs made needles from the thorns, rope and cloth from its fibre and roof thatch from the leaves. The sweet sap of the plant provided a drink called *pulque* and the worms which lived in the leaves were used in stews.

Only the nobles, who were given captured territories by the king, owned their own land. It was farmed by men who had sold themselves into slavery or men who did not belong to a clan and so had no right to land. Most people "borrowed" land from the clan. When a man married, his clan granted him a plot, which he kept until he died. The clan held annual meetings when the land was redistributed, always leaving some fallow.

Land was very precious, as it all had to be reclaimed from the lake. Every man helped to make new *chinampas* for his clan. First, lines of poles, with matting strung between them, were fixed in the lake bed. Then bundles of reeds and mats were weighted with stones and sunk between the poles. On this base the Aztecs piled mud from the lake bottom until the *chinampa* was formed. Trees planted round the edge helped to anchor the soil.

The soil from the lake bed was very fertile. Maize was the main crop and if this failed it meant starvation for all the Aztec people. They had special festivals to celebrate the harvest and even noblemen planted a few grains. As well as maize they grew beans, sage, amaranth, tomatoes, peppers and squash. All crops were manured with human dung collected from the public lavatories, boats moored along the canals.

Squash

Carrots

Sweet potato

Tomatoes

Maize

▲ The Aztec farmer grew these vegetables. Some, such as maize, were unknown in Europe.

Educating children

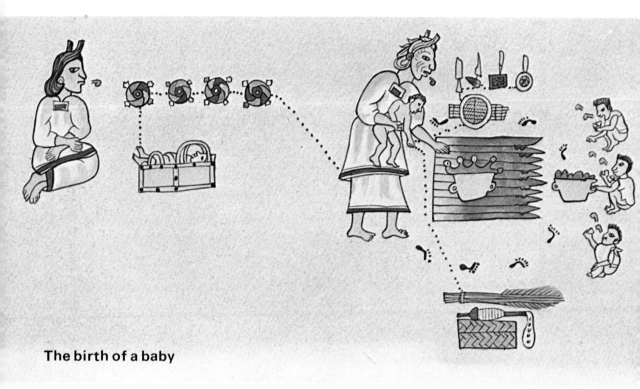

The birth of a baby

The Aztecs loved children and took their duties as parents very seriously. A midwife came to help with the birth. As soon as the baby was born she welcomed it and explained what sort of world it had come into. She told a boy that he must be a great warrior, feeding the sun god with the blood of his enemies. A girl, however, must stay at home, looking after her family.

Then the relatives arrived with presents and more good advice for the baby. The astrologer came to choose a lucky naming day and to foretell the baby's future. The Aztecs believed that your character was affected by your birth date. So, a child born on 6 Rabbit, for example, would probably be a drunkard, since Rabbit was the sign of drunkenness. The astrologer tried to remedy this kind of situation by choosing a luckier day to name the child.

On the chosen day, four small boys were invited to the house. While they ate honeycakes, the midwife made offerings to the gods and laid the baby on a mat. If it were a boy, she put tiny copies of his father's tools and a shield by him. A girl received a little work basket, a spindle and a broom. The midwife showed the baby how to use them, then told the baby its name. The four boys ran off to shout the new name through the streets. Relatives enjoyed the feasting and made long speeches on the hardship of life.

▲ This Aztec drawing shows the first steps in a baby's life. On the left the mother tells the newborn baby its duties in life. The four circles above show that four days have passed since this baby was born. The artist has put in the tools for a boy at the top and a girl below. You can see children using them on the opposite page.

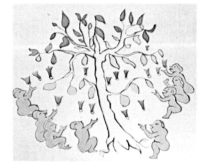

▲ This is an Aztec drawing of a children's story. Parents told their children stories about the time before they were born. Babies lived in a kind of paradise, eating the fruit of the mannaba tree, until it was time to be born.

► These drawings show parents teaching and punishing their children. Craftsmen taught their own sons. On the left a boy learns woodcarving, and on the right another boy makes jewellery.

► The boys learn painting, on the left, and goldworking. They are encouraged by the wise and gentle words of their father, which are drawn as blue scrolls coming from his mouth.

► Small boys carried loads for their fathers, while girls stayed at home, learning to cook and look after the house. The blue dots show the child's age, and the circles show how many tortillas he was allowed each day.

► While boys learned to fish in the lake, girls learned to weave. Disobedient children were pricked with thorns or held over a fire of burning peppers to make their eyes sting.

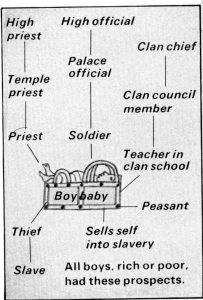

High priest
High official
Clan chief
Palace official
Temple priest
Clan council member
Priest
Soldier
Teacher in clan school
Boy baby
Peasant
Thief
Sells self into slavery
Slave
All boys, rich or poor, had these prospects.

Wives and mothers

Girls married at about sixteen and boys at twenty. In theory, men could have as many wives as they could afford, but most men settled for one. When the parents had decided on a suitable bride for their son, they employed a matchmaker to approach her parents. Young couples sometimes married in secret, but parents seemed to accept this quite happily. After the simple ceremony the singing, dancing and feasting lasted all night. Old people took the opportunity to make long speeches full of good advice for the couple.

▼ An Aztec painting of a marriage ceremony. In a procession of friends, the matchmaker carries the bride on her back to the groom's house. Inside, watched by their parents, she marries the couple by tying the corners of their cloaks together.

Herbal cures

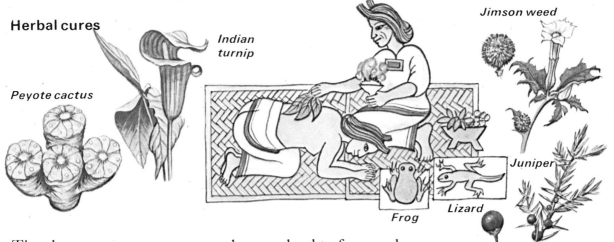

Peyote cactus

Indian turnip

Jimson weed

Frog

Lizard

Juniper

The clan gave every young couple some land to farm and build a house on. The wife raised the children, wove their clothes, helped with the harvest and sold extra produce in the market. When the children were grown up she could work as a midwife, a matchmaker, or a healer. This was an important and difficult job. The healer had to know how to use magic to find out whether an illness was caused by an enemy or by the gods as punishment. She had to know the right prayers and spells to say and the herbal medicines for each disease.

▲ The Aztecs used twelve hundred herbs to cure illnesses. Scientific tests show that many of these are very useful for reducing fever and stopping bleeding. Other cures, like eating roast lizard for a swollen face, did not work so well!

◄ Every woman wove her own cloth from cotton, which she combed and spun into thread. She then wove the thread into cloth on a belt loom. Cactus thorn needles were used for sewing, and women dyed their cloth with vegetable dyes. Very poor people used cactus fibre to weave their clothes.

25

Hairstyles

Married woman

Unmarried girl

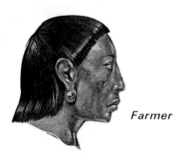

Warrior

Farmer

▲ Every class had its own hair style. Married women plaited their hair, winding the plaits round their head so that the ends stuck out at each side. Unmarried girls wore their hair loose.

This young man has tied up his hair to show that he is an experienced warrior, while the simple hairstyle of the man below shows that he is a farmer.

Clothes and appearance

For the Aztecs, clothes were a way of showing a person's rank, so there were very strict laws about who could wear what. An ordinary citizen's loincloth and cloak had to be of plain undyed maguey-fibre cloth. If he was caught wearing sandals in the palace he was put to death. As well as woven feather cloaks, nobles wore cotton cloaks with borders of precious stones. Craftsmen dyed the raw cotton green, blue, yellow and black with leaves and bark, red with crushed cochineal insects, and purple with the froth of a sea snail. They wove the yarn into geometrical patterns and designs of birds and flowers. As an extra touch, some cloaks were embroidered with gold thread. For winter, rabbit fur was woven into the cotton cloth.

The Aztecs loved jewellery, but there were also strict laws about this. For instance, to wear a crystal nose-plug when you were not entitled to it was punishable by death. Most people pierced their ears to hold plugs of shell or polished stones. Nobles were allowed to wear gold and carved precious stones in their lower lips to show their high rank.

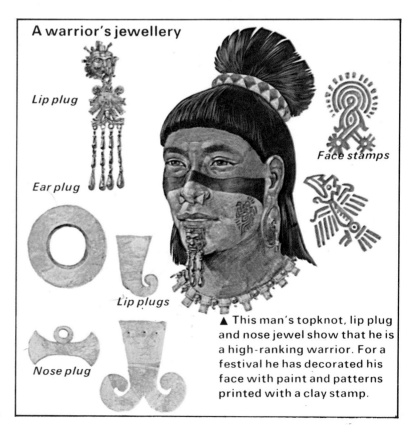

A warrior's jewellery

Lip plug

Ear plug

Face stamps

Lip plugs

Nose plug

▲ This man's topknot, lip plug and nose jewel show that he is a high-ranking warrior. For a festival he has decorated his face with paint and patterns printed with a clay stamp.

It did not take long for a farmer to dress. He slept in his loincloth. In the morning he picked up his blanket and draped it under one arm, knotted it on the other shoulder and was ready. He did not need to shave, and plucked out the odd hairs that grew with tweezers.

Cloth was woven on a belt loom in lengths about 90 centimetres wide. One length, sewn up the sides, with a hole for her head, made a woman's blouse. Another length wound round her waist and secured with an embroidered belt made her skirt. She had to walk with tiny steps so that the skirt would not flap open and show her knees.

▲ Aztecs prized bright feathers more highly than gold. Young nobles wore brightly-coloured cloaks and headdresses and carried fans and bunches of sweet smelling flowers. For dances they painted their bodies. Girls liked to paint their faces yellow with crushed insects and to dye their teeth red, although their parents disapproved. Girls also used the pottery stamps to decorate their faces with patterns.

27

Sacred games

▲ A Maya ball court at Chichen Itza. The Aztecs copied the Maya courts, but built theirs smaller.

Netball and basketball come from the ancient American game of *tlachtli*. No one knows when the Indians first discovered how to make rubber sap into bouncing balls, but the game was played long before the Aztecs came to Mexico. Like all their games, the ball game had a religious meaning. The stone court was a copy of the heavens where, they believed, the gods played ball with the stars. Only nobles were allowed to play, but everyone came to watch and bet on their favourite team. There were two teams and the aim was to hit the ball through the opponents' stone ring, which was just wide enough for the ball to go through. This was so difficult that a player who scored a "goal" won outright, and had the right to demand the clothes and possessions of the audience. However, people usually managed to scramble away before the player could catch them.

The nobles also enjoyed music, singing and plays, and all rich households kept their own orchestra and entertainers.

Sometimes, the Aztecs would pass the time by gambling. They offered prayers to Five Flower, the god of gambling, in the hope that they would be lucky. Some people gambled away all their possessions, even their clothes, and were forced to sell themselves as slaves.

▲ This competition was only for boys training as warriors. The idea was to scramble up the greasy pole to reach the sweet dough figure of a god at the top.

▶ *Patolli* was the favourite game of ordinary Aztecs. They played on a mat with 52 squares, with red and blue counters and beans marked as dice. It was rather like Lotto, and a player won when he got three counters in a row.

▼ The *tlachtli* players were only allowed to hit the ball with their knees, elbows or hips. They had to throw themselves on the stone floor to do this, and wore leather gloves and padding to protect themselves.

Learning to be a priest

▲ Quetzalcoatl, the god of priests, was always drawn with his symbol, the quetzal bird.

1 The cleverest boys went to the *calmecac* or priests' school at the age of eight. They lived on tortillas and water, slept on the bare floor and fasted for days.

4 Every morning the boys had to prick their ears and tongue with thorns to please the gods, and sacrifice a quail to offer its beating heart to the sun.

5 When he was twenty, a priest could leave to marry. Then he might work as a palace scribe, a doctor, or a soothsayer. One of his tasks was to choose the luckiest day to name a new baby and to foretell its future.

2 Each night the boys got up twice to pray. At night they collected insects to make the priests' black body paint.

3 School priests taught the boys to read and write, to make herbal medicines and to foretell eclipses, droughts and famines by watching the stars. They also learned the right songs and prayers for each of the many gods.

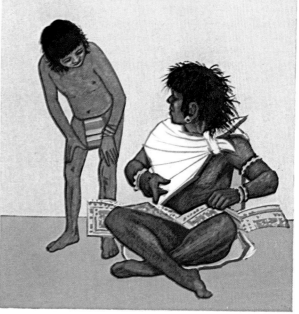

6 To perform his vital job, the priest had to carry out the right ceremonies, keep the temple fires lit and make sacrifices at the right time.

Watching the stars

► The god of the Evening Star watches the night sky from the temple platform. On the left are the crossed sticks through which priests observed the stars at sunset, midnight and dawn.

▼ People took their names from the day on which they were born. This is the Aztec sign for the name 6 Monkey Shoulder-cape. The triangle and crossed bands mean shoulder-cape. Beside this is the monkey head with six dots. Since several babies might be born on the same day, each child was also given a personal name.

Only the priests trained in astrology could read the sacred calendar. No one dared name a child, go on a journey or start a new piece of work without consulting a priest, for the Aztecs believed that there were lucky and unlucky days. 7 Flower was lucky for painters and 1 House for midwives. Merchants travelled on 1 Snake. A child born on 1 Ocelot would die as a prisoner of war. 4 Dog meant good fortune, but a child born on 2 Rabbit would become a drunkard and there was nothing he could do about it.

The work of the astrologer-priest was much more complicated. As well as the day-name and number, he had to take into account the hour of the day and the god who controlled each group of thirteen days. Using the sacred calendar, and watching the stars every night, the astrologer-priest was able to advise the king on important matters such as when to go to war, when to expect a drought or when the gods needed more sacrifices. Priests therefore held a great deal of power over the Aztec people.

The Aztec calendar

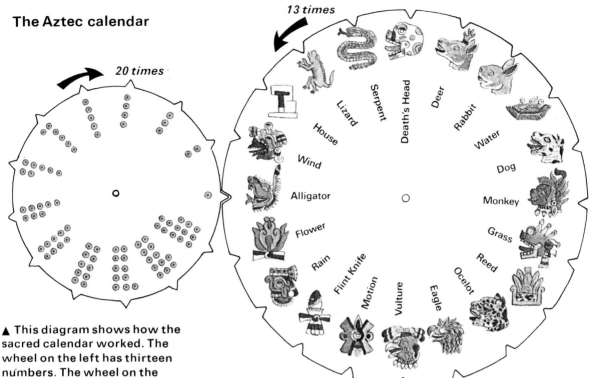

20 times

13 times

Lizard · Serpent · Death's Head · Deer · Rabbit · Water · House · Wind · Alligator · Flower · Rain · Flint Knife · Motion · Vulture · Eagle · Ocelot · Reed · Grass · Monkey · Dog

▲ This diagram shows how the sacred calendar worked. The wheel on the left has thirteen numbers. The wheel on the right has twenty named days. The wheels turn so that each day fits in with a number. The year starts on 1 Alligator. The next day is 2 Wind, and so on.

After thirteen days the left-hand wheel has come round to 1 again to begin a new week. 1 is now opposite Ocelot, so that the week starts on 1 Ocelot then turns to 2 Eagle and so on. In this week, Alligator falls on day 8.

After 260 days, the left-hand wheel has turned twenty times, and the calendar starts again on 1 Alligator.

▶ The solar calendar of 365 days and the sacred calendar of 260 days ran together. The first days of each calendar came together once every 52 years. This cycle of 52 years was very important to the Aztecs. They feared that, on that day, every 52 years, the world might end, and prepared themselves for this by throwing away all their possessions.

By 600 BC, the Maya had calculated that there were 365.242 days in a year. The Aztecs adopted this solar year and divided it into eighteen weeks of twenty days, with five unlucky extra days at the end of each year. They also used a sacred calendar of 260 days to foretell the future. This had twenty weeks of thirteen days. Aztec dates were a mixture of the two calendars.

Offerings to the gods

▲ This sacrificial knife has an Eagle Warrior as its handle.

◀ This Aztec painting shows a priest sacrificing a man to the gods. Another victim lies at the bottom of the temple steps.

▲ The Volador Ceremony. The ropes unwind as the men spiral to the ground, imitating the flight of the gods. Each man circles the pole 13 times, the number of days in a week.

The Aztecs believed that the gods had sacrificed themselves to create the sun. It was therefore the Aztecs' duty to feed the gods with "sacred water" or blood. Each month there was a festival to make an offering to the gods. At the Festival of the God of Spring, for example, a young man was shot with arrows. His blood fertilized the soil.

Not all festivals were gruesome. There were some where people danced and sang to the gods in the main square. At one festival, small boys hid with bags of leaves, jumping out to wallop women as they walked past. At the Festival of the Lords the king gave a feast for the whole city.

The most important festival was the New Fire Ceremony, which took place every 52 years. People went to the Hill of New Fire. Just before dawn the chief priest sacrificed a man. As the priest kindled the new fire, the sun rose. Everyone cheered. The world was safe again.

Temples and shrines

▲ The Spaniards destroyed all the temples in Tenochtitlan. This is a smaller temple, that still survives at Tenayuca. In designing their temples, the Aztecs copied the buildings of much older civilizations.

The Aztecs built their temples from huge blocks of stone brought from the mountains around the Valley of Mexico. Craftsmen carved great serpents' heads and eagle warriors around the walls. The temples were raised as high as possible, so the Aztecs could be near to their sky gods. On the platform at the top of one stood two shrines, one dedicated to Tlaloc, the god of rain, and the other to Blue Hummingbird. The Spaniards destroyed the temples, but left this description of what they had seen: "Inside the shrine was a great statue of Blue Hummingbird, his face and body covered with gold and jewels. There were some smoking braziers of their incense in which they were burning the hearts of three Indians."

All roads led to the great temple of Blue Hummingbird in the middle of the city. When the Spaniards arrived in Tenochtitlan, they saw the temple towering 30 metres above the two-storeyed houses around it. As the people watched from the square below, the religious processions climbed the great stone staircases, disappearing from view at the top. People who had been chosen as offerings to the gods were then sacrificed on the temple platform.

▶ The Aztecs believed that they should build a new temple every 52 years to thank their gods that the world had not ended. Instead of pulling down the old temple, they built a new one over the top. Each temple was therefore bigger and more imposing than the last. In Tenochtitlan, the great temple had been enlarged five times.

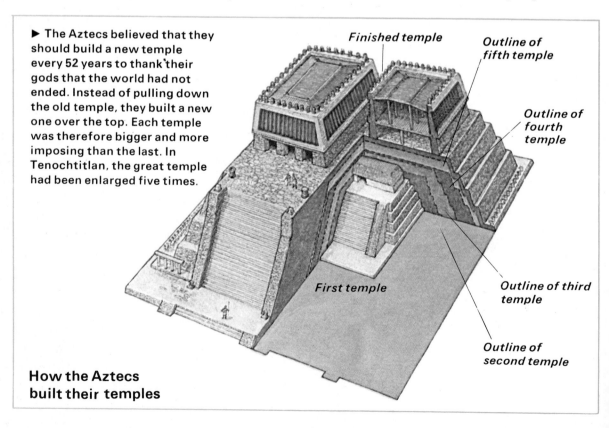

Finished temple

Outline of fifth temple

Outline of fourth temple

Outline of third temple

First temple

Outline of second temple

How the Aztecs built their temples

On the temple platform the smoke from incense and burning hearts rose to the gods. The priests' black body paint contained drugs which enabled them to dance and sing for hours without getting tired.

Arts and crafts

▼ A Spanish drawing showing a featherworker. He dips the feathers in glue and sticks them to a backing of stiffened cloth.

Featherworking

Featherworking was a family business. While the children prepared glue from bat dung, the wife sorted and dyed the backing feathers that would not show in the finished product. To make a shield the craftsman first drew a design and made a stencil. With this, he transferred the design to a piece of cloth glued to cactus fibres. He cut the dyed feathers to shape and stuck them·on to the cloth. Then he glued the cloth to a board backing. When this was dry he applied the final layer of feathers, outlining the pattern with thin strips of gold. The most expensive feathers came from the sacred green quetzal bird and turquoise hummingbird.

Aztec craftsmen

The Aztec craftsmen learned their crafts from the descendants of the Toltecs, whose civilization had come to an end long before the Aztecs came to Mexico. Craftsmen lived in their own part of the city, worshipping their own gods and passing on their special skills only to their children. Much of their work was for the king. They took the tribute sent from conquered cities and made headdresses, cloaks and jewels. The king then rewarded great warriors with these gifts.

It took a long time for a sculptor to finish a piece in jade, crystal or obsidian as he had such poor tools. He cut out the rough shape by rubbing a strip of raw hide roughened with sand and water over the stone. He had only a soft copper knife and ground flint with which to put in the details. He finished off by polishing the piece with sand, then with cane to give it a high gloss.

▼ The Aztecs loved flowers and carved this beautiful statue of their God of Flowers. He was also the god of music, song and pleasure. Here, this happy god is singing and accompanying himself with a rattle in each hand. However, these rattles are now missing.

▲ This carving, over two metres in length, is made from a huge block of red cornelian. It stood for the name of a place, Chapultepec, or Grasshopper Hill.

▼ The Spaniards were not interested in the beautiful Aztec craftsmanship, and melted down all the gold objects they found. This tiny mask of the god Xipe Totec was found in a tomb in 1932.

◄ This Spanish drawing shows a gold worker melting down gold to make a pendant.

Goldworking

The goldsmith made round objects by the lost-wax method. He made a model in clay, covered it with beeswax and coated it with more clay. He heated the model to make the wax run out through a hole in the bottom. He poured in molten gold, let it cool, then broke open the clay shell.

The young warrior

Shield

▲ Blue Hummingbird, god of war, patron of the school.

Club

▲ The Aztecs' main weapon was a wooden club edged with razor-sharp blades of volcanic glass.

Spear

Spear thrower

◀ Warriors used an *atlatl* or wooden thrower to give their spears extra thrust. Shields were decorated with feathers and mosaic.

1 At the age of eight, boys were taken to the *telpochcalli*, the clan's boarding school, to train as warriors.

4 They practised combat with wooden weapons. Later, they followed the warriors great distances to battle, carrying their food.

2 All the boys led a tough life. They learned to be humble and obedient by doing lowly jobs like digging canals and sweeping the temples. Peasant boys were allowed home for a few hours each day to help their fathers.

3 Boys learned the songs and dances of their religion and the city's laws. Lazy boys were punished with thorns.

6 Even a peasant boy who distinguished himself in battle could be rewarded by the king with goods and noble rank.

A young warrior's aim was to capture three emies alive and become a "Master of Cuts" d tie up his hair. The best warriors joined the gle and jaguar warriors. When a warrior died battle, his soul went to a special heaven ar the sun.

The Aztec conquerors

The Aztecs won their huge empire by war. When the king and council decided to take over a city, they first sent ambassadors who stated their demands. The city must trade with them, worship the Aztec god Blue Hummingbird, and send gifts to Mexico every year. They gave the city three chances, returning to repeat their demands every twenty days.

▲ Aztecs rushed into battle with as much noise as possible, shouting and blowing clay whistles. Commanders gave orders by beating on small drums hung round their necks.

Every time the city refused to give in, the Aztecs gave the people a gift of spears and shields so they would not be helpless in the destruction to follow. If the city still held out after this grim warning, the Aztec priests chose a lucky day and the two armies met at noon. The battle was short and fierce, ending when the Aztec army reached the enemy's temple. The people knew then that the Aztec god was stronger than their own. Then the bargaining began to decide how much tribute the city should send to Tenochtitlan each year. Surgeons sewed up the terrible wounds caused by the obsidian blades and scribes counted the number of live sacrificial victims captured.

In peaceful times the Aztecs still needed victims to sacrifice to their gods. Then they arranged a "War of Flowers" with another city. Priests watched and stopped the battle when enough men had been captured from each side. The bravest men ran naked into battle with only a net to capture live victims for sacrifice.

▲ There was no professional army. Every boy trained as a warrior and went to war in his clan led by his clan chief. Untrained warriors, wearing padded cotton tunics stiffened with brine, followed experienced warriors into battle.

43

Montezuma's empire

In 1427 the Aztecs were a small, poor tribe paying tribute to another kingdom. In less than a hundred years they were masters of an empire which stretched from the shores of the Pacific to the Gulf of Mexico and included five hundred towns and fifteen million people.

They were not interested in changing the way of life of the people they conquered. As long as the town agreed to worship Blue Hummingbird, to send its serious law cases to Tenochtitlan to be judged and to pay its tribute, it was left in peace.

Tribute was a form of taxation. Detailed lists were drawn up showing exactly what goods each town should pay the Aztec state. Some of the tribute was kept by the king, some was given to the clans to share out and some went to warriors as a reward for brave deeds.

▲ Every year Aztec officials travelled to the towns of the empire to collect tribute. The amount of tribute had been agreed during the peace talks after the town was captured. Scribes kept careful records of each collection. It was this tribute that made the Aztecs so rich—and so hated.

Jade beads

20 bags cochineal dye

400 bags red peppers

Black beans

400 bunches feathers

Tropical birds

Warrior costumes

Jaguar skins

Shields

Blankets

◄ The Aztecs kept records of tribute, or taxes, that other towns had to pay them. This is what a page from a tribute roll looked like. Beside some goods the Aztecs wrote symbols to show how many of each kind were required.

A tribute list

The merchants were different from other Aztecs. They were only interested in gaining wealth and travelled throughout the empire with loads of manufactured goods to barter. The king found them very useful as spies, as they brought news of wealthy towns and the size of their armies.

Merchants lived in their own district of the city. They hid their wealth and pretended to be poor, going barefoot and in plain cloaks in the streets, for only nobles were allowed to dress in fine clothes. Only in their own homes could they wear feathers and jewels, and enjoy the treasure they had brought back from their travels.

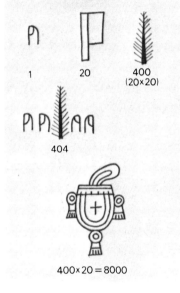

▼ These are the symbols for Aztec numbers. You can see how they were used in the tribute list opposite.

1   20   400 (20×20)

404

400×20 = 8000

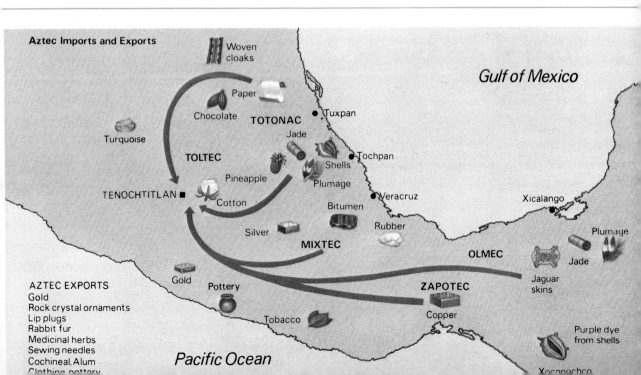

Aztec Imports and Exports

Woven cloaks

Gulf of Mexico

Paper

Chocolate

TOTONAC

Tuxpan

Jade

Turquoise

TOLTEC

Tochpan

Shells

Pineapple

Plumage

TENOCHTITLAN ■

Cotton

Bitumen

Veracruz

Xicalango

Silver

Rubber

Plumage

MIXTEC

OLMEC

Jade

Gold

Pottery

ZAPOTEC

Jaguar skins

AZTEC EXPORTS
Gold
Rock crystal ornaments
Lip plugs
Rabbit fur
Medicinal herbs
Sewing needles
Cochineal, Alum
Clothing, pottery

Tobacco

Copper

Purple dye from shells

Pacific Ocean

Xoconochco

Montezuma the King

The Aztec king shared control of the city with Snake Woman, his chief official. As king, Montezuma was mainly concerned with foreign affairs, but had to consult his council on such matters. His duties were to receive tribute from conquered cities, reward warriors and distribute grain to his people when the harvests failed.

▲ Nobles carried Montezuma through the streets in a litter. No one was allowed to look at his face. Inside the palace, nobles had to approach him barefoot and in shabby cloaks. He spoke to them through an official, never directly.

Although his father was king, Montezuma was brought up like other boys. He trained as a priest in the *calmecac*, wearing tattered cloaks and fasting, learning how to read the sacred books and watch the stars. Then he trained as a warrior and by eighteen he was a "Master of Cuts" and a qualified priest. When his uncle became king Montezuma served as an army commander. Montezuma was elected king in 1503.

This changed his life completely. He moved into a huge new palace and married princesses from every tribe in the empire. His ambition was to make his empire as great as that of the ancient Toltecs. His armies conquered vast lands and he filled his palace with musicians and Toltec craftsmen. He tried to live like the Toltec kings, which made him even more remote from his people.

▲ This is Montezuma's royal headdress, made from precious stones and quetzal feathers. Cortes was amazed by its beauty and sent it to Charles V of Spain, who gave it to his Austrian nephew. It is now in an Austrian museum, and is almost the only piece of Aztec feather-work that still exists.

▶ In one part of the palace was Montezuma's private zoo, a collection of animals from all over the empire, sent back by his conquering armies. It included parrots, eagles, jaguars and monkeys.

Defeat and conquest

▶ In the year before the Spanish Conquest the Aztecs saw terrible omens. People heard a woman crying in the streets at night for her dead sons. From his palace roof Montezuma studies a comet that appeared in the eastern sky every night.

Cortes and his Spanish adventurers landed at Vera Cruz in 1519. By an extraordinary coincidence, this was the last year of the Aztecs' 52-year cycle and the year in which they feared that the god Quetzalcoatl would return from exile to destroy them. Montezuma therefore believed that the Spaniards were gods and did not dare fight them. When his magic spells failed to stop them, he welcomed them into the city. He did not even resist when they took him prisoner. But when the Spanish soldiers fired on a religious procession, the Aztecs attacked. Cortes managed to escape, but later returned with reinforcements, bringing boats in sections overland. They surrounded the city and waited for the Aztecs to surrender.

▲ One day some fishermen brought Montezuma a bird with a mirror in its head. In it he saw warriors riding on monstrous deer. When he called his soothsayers to explain the omen, the bird disappeared.

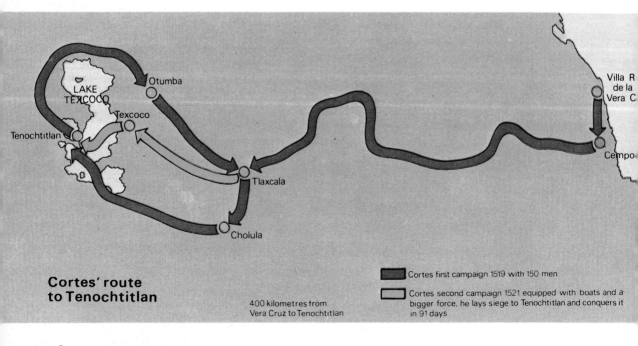

Otumba

LAKE TEXCOCO

Texcoco

Tenochtitlan

Tlaxcala

Cholula

Villa R de la Vera C

Cempo

Cortes' route to Tenochtitlan

400 kilometres from Vera Cruz to Tenochtitlan

Cortes first campaign 1519 with 150 men

Cortes second campaign 1521 equipped with boats and a bigger force, he lays siege to Tenochtitlan and conquers it in 91 days

How the Aztecs were defeated

How did 600 men conquer an empire? Part of the answer is in the picture above. The Aztecs' beautiful costumes and obsidian spears were no match for armour, guns and cannon. They had never seen horses and the cavalry charges terrified them. The Spaniards were also helped by other tribes happy to be free of Aztec domination.

The Aztecs had a different attitude to war from the Spaniards. Instead of killing the enemy, they wasted time taking captives to be sacrificed to their god of war. When the Spaniards entered the city they were horrified to find the heads of soldiers and horses on the skull rack in the square.

▼ A portrait of Cortes.

Prices, weights and measures

The Aztecs did not have money as we know it. They simply exchanged goods of equal value. A village might barter its extra pottery for another village's flint knives. People took their produce to market to exchange it for what they needed. Cocoa beans were used to even out small differences in value. Beans were easy to carry and everyone liked cocoa.

There was no detailed system of weights and measures either. A "load" was the weight one man could carry comfortably on his back. They measured length by the human body. The distance across a man's hand, the distance from one outstretched hand to the other and the distance from the ground to his upstretched fingertips all served for measuring length.

Prices

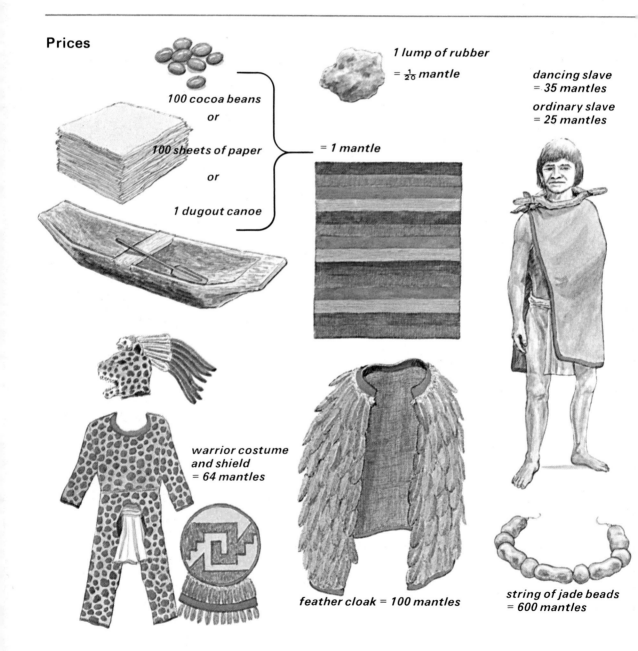

1 lump of rubber = $\frac{1}{20}$ mantle

dancing slave = 35 mantles

ordinary slave = 25 mantles

100 cocoa beans
or
100 sheets of paper
or
1 dugout canoe

= 1 mantle

warrior costume and shield = 64 mantles

feather cloak = 100 mantles

string of jade beads = 600 mantles

The gods

The Aztecs worshipped many gods, who each looked after a different part of life. They believed that the gods watched them constantly and would become angry if the people did not carry out the right sacrifices and festivals at the right time. The Aztecs therefore tried to win the favour of the gods by sacrificing many prisoners.

▲ Tonatiuh, the sun god

When the Aztecs came to Mexico in the twelfth century they were hunters, and worshipped sky gods: Blue Hummingbird, god of the noonday sun, Coatlicue his mother, and Tezcatlipoca, god of night. They settled in the Valley of Mexico and learned writing and astrology from the Toltecs. They began to worship the Toltec god of learning, Quetzalcoatl. When farming became important, and the Aztecs needed rain, they began to worship the Toltec god of rain, Tlaloc, and the earth goddesses who make the plants grow. As their empire grew, they learned of new gods from other tribes and introduced them to their city to be honoured in festivals. A new temple had to be built for these gods next to the huge temple of Blue Hummingbird in the city.

The poor people, however, continued to worship their local gods, believing that these gods protected their harvests and food supplies. Each town or village had its own particular god, and each trade had its own patron god.

The Aztecs thought of the earth as a disc, surrounded by water. Each direction had a different heaven. Souls of warriors went to the paradise of the sun in the east. Souls of women who had died in childbirth went to the western earth-goddesses' paradise. Drowned people went to Tlaloc's spring paradise in the south. Everyone else travelled to the north, a region ruled by the Lord and Lady of Death. This fearsome couple wore masks made from human skulls and also ruled the hells below the earth.

▲ Coatlicue, Mother Earth

Aztec writing

Governing the empire needed an enormous amount of paperwork. This was all done by priests specially trained as scribes. They drew up maps, listed all tribute collected and kept records of legal decisions. Each clan had its own land records and each temple had a religious library.

Making paper

Stripping bark

Bark beater

The paper was made from the bark of the wild fig tree, soaked and beaten into sheets. It was coated with a chalky varnish and stuck together in strips of up to 11 metres. Each book was folded like a concertina and the scribe drew on both sides.

Reading a codex

The Aztecs had no alphabet, and simply wrote in pictures or glyphs. Just as we always write a word in the same way, they always drew a picture in the same way. A page of an Aztec book looks like a jumble of tiny pictures, but it was drawn according to very strict rules. It took a lot of training to be able to read and write them. Although Aztec books look complicated, the tiny pictures themselves are simple.

To show that something was farther away they drew it near the top of the page. If one man is drawn bigger than another, it means he is more important. Since the Aztecs did not have words, they had to *show* that a person was speaking. To do this they drew blue scrolls coming out of his mouth. The reader had to guess what he was saying by reading the rest of the pictures. A line of footprints on the page meant that a person was travelling somewhere.

Some things were easy to write in glyphs. A scribe might want to say that in the year 1 Flint, King Jade Feather conquered the city Burning Reed in the evening. To describe this story, he would draw a flint knife with a dot next to it (the year 1 Flint), a king's headdress with a green feather above it (King Jade Feather), a temple with an arrow in it (conquered), and below a reed and a fire (the city Burning Reed). At the top of the picture he drew a half circle with some stars sticking out of it to show that it was evening.

But there were some words that were impossible to say in glyphs because there

A Mexican codex

Glyphs

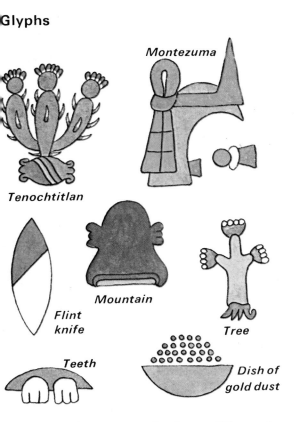

Montezuma

Tenochtitlan

Flint knife

Mountain

Tree

Teeth

Dish of gold dust

For example, if he wanted to show the city Quauhtitlan, he had to draw a tree with a set of teeth in its trunk. The city's name is not "tree-teeth", but the Aztec word for tree is *quauitl* and the word for teeth is *tlantli*. By putting the two words together you make a word that sounds like the word you want to say.

When the Spanish priests came to Mexico after the conquest, they became interested in the Aztecs' old way of life and encouraged them to draw pictures to record how they had lived before the Spanish invasion. Most of our knowledge of the Aztecs is based on these records.

Codex styles

The two pictures below show how the Aztecs' style of drawing changed after the conquest. The warrior on the left was painted before the conquest. He is outlined in black and filled in with bright, flat colours. From the details in the drawing we can build up an impression of who he is and what he does. The eagle warrior on the right was painted after the conquest and no longer tells us a great deal about him.

were no pictures to fit them. Then the artist had to think of another word that sounded the same. It was up to the reader to decide whether the picture meant the thing that was drawn or just something that sounded like it.

Mixtec-style warrior

Spanish-style warrior

Story of the Aztecs

1168

This is the traditional date when the Aztecs, a small hunting tribe, left their island home of Aztlan to the north of Mexico. After the destruction of the great civilization of the Toltecs in the Valley of Mexico, many tribes wandered in from the north, seeking land. The Aztecs were one of the last of these tribes. For over a hundred years they travelled, settling for a time, planting their harvest, and then being driven on.

1323

Finally the Aztec tribe arrived at some islands in the marshy Lake Texcoco. Here they saw the sign they had been promised by their god, Blue Hummingbird. The sign was an eagle with a snake in its beak, sitting on a cactus. They called the place Tenochtitlan and built their first reed huts round a temple to Blue Hummingbird. Since there was no food, they were forced to live off the frogs and waterbirds of the lake and had to pay tribute and fight as mercenary soldiers for the nearby kingdom of Azcapotzalco.

1427

Their chief, Itzcoatl, joined with three other tribute-paying towns to revolt against Azcapotzalco. After their victory the three towns, Tenochtitlan, Texcoco and Tlacópan, agreed to make an alliance to share in war expeditions to conquer more territory.

1440

Montezuma I began the construction of great aqueducts to bring fresh water from the mainland for the growing city. Soil was reclaimed from the lake bed to extend the island. As the city grew, Toltec craftsmen came to settle, bringing their knowledge of gold and feather-working. The Aztecs also learned from the Toltecs how to read the stars and calculate the calendar, and the Toltec gods Quetzalcoatl and Tlaloc were introduced into the Aztec religion. Montezuma conquered new land in the south and on the Gulf Coast and tribute of gold dust, cocoa and cotton poured into the city.

▼ The Aztecs building Tenochtitlan.

1469

Axayacatl conquered the neighbouring island town of Tlatelolco for its market. The empire extended to the Pacific coast.

▲ Aztec warriors conquer neighbouring tribes.

1503

Montezuma II became king. He broke up the alliance with the two other towns by electing his own choice as king of Texcoco. The prince Ixtilxochitl fled to the hills.

1519

Hernan Cortes, the Spanish adventurer, who had been living in Cuba, persuaded the Spanish government to let him lead an expedition to Mexico. His aim was to convert the Indians to Christianity and to seek gold. He landed on the coast of Mexico at the place from which the god Quetzalcoatl had left six hundred years before. Montezuma believed that Cortes was the god returning and tried to keep him away by magic, but then welcomed him into the city. Cortes took Montezuma

hostage. However, the Spaniards then mistook a religious procession for a revolt, and began a battle with the Aztecs. The Spaniards were forced to flee by night, but were seen, and only a hundred men reached safety. Many men drowned in the lake weighed down by their armour and looted gold.

1521

Cortes returned to Tlaxcala to summon reinforcements from the coast. He built parts of twelve shallow-bottomed boats, which the Spaniards assembled at the lakeside. For three months they besieged the city, the population dying of disease and starvation, until the Spaniards broke through and raised the Spanish flag from the temple platform. The Aztecs were defeated. The Spaniards found little gold. However, they discovered the king's tribute lists. Using these as a map, they set off to march through Central America in search of treasure.

▼ The Spaniards raise their flag on the temple platform.

The world in the sixteenth century

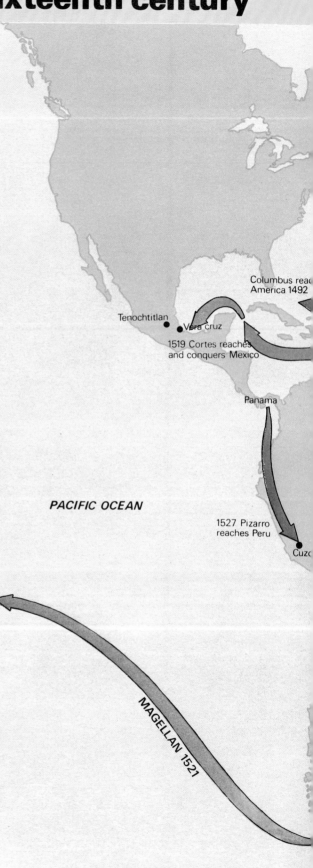

As you can see from this map, Mexico was not the only country to fall before European invaders. In 1492, Columbus sailed west from Spain to try and find a sea-route to India. Instead, he discovered the continent of America. Until this time, people had believed that the world was flat. In 1522, Magellan completed his historic voyage round the world which finally proved that the world was round.

As soon as word reached Europe of the great lands to the west, expeditions quickly set sail from Seville and Lisbon to claim lands for Spain and Portugal, and to search for gold, wealth and glory for their countries. So great was the rivalry between the two countries that the Pope was obliged to step in and settle the matter. He divided the New World into two. Spain was to have the west, while Portugal could explore the continent of Africa and lands to the east.

In 1519, Cortes reached the Valley of Mexico and completely destroyed the Aztec civilization. Soon after this, Pizarro travelled south from Panama to Cuzco, high in the Andes, and conquered the Incas. From that time onwards, the story of the peoples of America is a sad one. In Mexico, the Spaniards despised the descendants of the Aztecs and their neighbouring tribes and deprived them of their rights and freedom. Spanish settlers arrived, taking all the land and wealth for themselves. It was only after a revolution in 1910 that all the people of Mexico finally gained equal rights and equal status.

Columbus reac[hed] America 1492

Tenochtitlan

Vera cruz

1519 Cortes reache[s] and conquers Mexico

Panama

PACIFIC OCEAN

1527 Pizarro reaches Peru

Cuzc[o]

MAGELLAN 1521

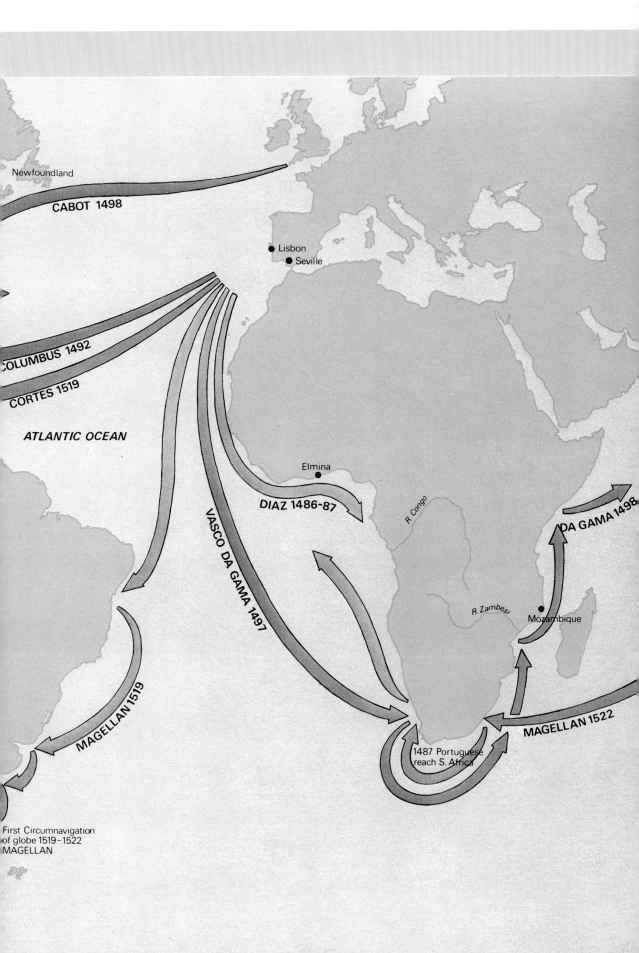

Newfoundland

CABOT 1498

● Lisbon
● Seville

COLUMBUS 1492

CORTES 1519

ATLANTIC OCEAN

Elmina

DIAZ 1486-87

R. Congo

DA GAMA 1498

VASCO DA GAMA 1497

R. Zambesi

Mozambique

MAGELLAN 1519

MAGELLAN 1522

1487 Portuguese
reach S. Africa

First Circumnavigation
of globe 1519–1522
MAGELLAN

World history AD 1100 to 1500

	Aztecs	Europe	Asia
AD 1100	The Aztecs, one of the Chichimec group of Indians, take advantage of the downfall of the Toltec empire in AD 1000, and move into the Valley of Mexico. The Aztecs continue their search for land. They live in one place after another while pioneers find new sites to plant the harvest.	Independent city-states emerge in Italy. The north German cities become great trading centres and Constantinople is established as the centre of European culture. Thomas Becket is murdered at Canterbury Cathedral. Universities are established at Oxford and in Paris.	Genghis Khan extends the Mongol Empire from Manchu to the Caucasus, and begins t invasion of Russia. Under the Sung dynasty, fine porcelain is produced. The Ch'in dynasty gains cont of much of China.
AD 1200	They settle at Chapultepec but after stealing some Tepanec women, most of the tribe are defeated and become the slaves of the Tepanecs. Some Aztecs escape to the marshy islands of Lake Texcoco.	The Magna Carta is signed. St Francis founds the Franciscan Order. Mongols invade Poland and Hungary. Edward I conquers Wales, but the Scots rebel and ally with France.	The Mongols invade Russia, and are defeated in the west, control east Russia and exact wealth and taxes. Genghis K▮ invades China and Kublai Kh▮ sets up his capital at Peking, welcoming traveller Marco P▮
AD 1300	The Aztecs distinguish themselves in battle and the Tepanecs reward them with a princess for their chief. Instead of marrying her, they sacrifice her, and are driven out by the horrified Tepanecs. The Aztecs join the rest of their tribe and found the city of Tenochtitlan in the lake.	England is defeated by the Scots at the Battle of Bannockburn, and the Hundred Years War between England and France begins. The Black Death sweeps through Europe. In England, the Peasants' Revolt is suppressed. Portugal gains independence from Spain.	Under the Mongols, the centr▮ state of Moscow is created, b▮ the Prince of Moscow drives the Mongols out. The Mongols are driven out o China, which is then closed t▮ foreigners. The Mongols invade India.
AD 1400	They combine with three other towns to defeat the Tepanecs and take over their empire. They begin the conquest of the Valley and amass great wealth. They build a great empire and elect Montezuma I as their Chief Speaker.	England is defeated by the French armies, led by Joan of Arc. She is later burnt at the stake. The Italian Renaissance reaches its height, producing such artists as Da Vinci and Botticelli. Gutenberg invents the printing press and the Hapsburgs reign supreme in central Europe.	Tamerlane's empire collapses and India, Persia and Afghanistan gain independer Religious conflict breaks out between Hindus and Moslem in India. Vasco da Gama reaches Indi▮ Civil war breaks out in Japan.
AD 1500	Montezuma II becomes ruler of the Aztecs. Cortes lands at Vera Cruz and begins his campaign against the Aztecs with the help of enemy tribes. Montezuma is killed and the empire is destroyed.	The Moors are finally driven out of Spain, who conquers new lands in the Americas. Luther and Calvin preach against the Papacy and åre active in the Reformation. Copernicus makes discoveries in astronomy. Drake destroys the Spanish Armada.	Ivan the Terrible conquers Siberia, and the Russian Chu▮ becomes independent. The Mogul empire unites Ind▮ in a great civilization. Portugal establishes trading posts in India and her ships visit Japan. The Dutch begin a spice trade with the Spice Islands.

rica	Near East	America	

			AD 1100
pt is ruled by the Fatimid asty, Moslems, who are tile to the Seljuk Turks, but o support them in their fight egain Jerusalem from the saders. Cairo and Alexandria le with the Far East. adin becomes ruler of Egypt conquers Jerusalem.	Crusader states are founded along the coast of Syria, with castles. The Crusaders take Jerusalem, then lose it to Saladin, the ruler of Egypt and Syria, who allows Christian pilgrims to visit the shrines there.	Northern hunting Chichimec tribes move into the Valley of Mexico and settle there. The Inca civilization grows and builds huge stone fortresses.	

			AD 1200
ypt and Venice negotiate a de treaty. The Fifth Crusade Egypt is defeated, and Louis of France is killed. e Sultan of Egypt defeats a ongol invasion. e Mandingo empire is ablished, with its centre at nbuktu.	Jerusalem is won back by the Crusaders, who are again defeated, losing their Crusader states, and forced to retreat to Cyprus. The Mongols invade the Near East and destroy Baghdad.	The Chichimec tribes establish small kingdoms in the Valley and fight constantly to extend their territory. Many marry into the noble Toltec families. Raids by Navaho Indians in the American south-west destroy the Cliff Dweller culture.	

			AD 1300
st Africa becomes united in Mandingo empire. The end of Prester John, a ristian king in East Africa, eads. ypt suffers the Black Death, d Alexandria is captured by king of Cyprus. e Arabs develop a slave de along the east coast.	The Turks establish the Ottoman Empire and conquer Greece. Turkish power spreads in eastern Europe.	The Inca empire extends in Peru. Civil war breaks out among the Mayas on the Yucatan peninsula, and their civilization begins to decline.	

			AD 1400
e Portuguese explore the ast of West Africa and found a ding post on the Guinea ast. They sail up the Congo er and convert the king of the ngo empire to Christianity. rtholomew Diaz reaches the pe of Good Hope and Vasco Gama rounds the Cape.	The Mongols conquer Turkish lands in Asia and destroy the Turkish army. The Turks in Greece recover, invade Hungary and capture Constantinople, which they re-name Istanbul.	The Incas build military roads throughout the empire and navigate along the coasts. Christopher Columbus reaches the New World. The Pope gives Spain the right to explore west and Portugal to explore east of Europe. John Cabot reaches Newfound-land and claims it for England.	**AD**

			AD 1500
e Portuguese found ozambique and explore the mbezi River. e British begin the export of ves from West Africa to the w World. ain captures Tunis from the rks. rtuguese missionaries settle Ethiopia but are expelled.	The Turks extend their empire to north-west India and Arabia. Turkish sea power is broken by Spain and Venice at the Battle of Lepanto.	Spain conquers the Inca and Aztec empires, reducing the Indians to slavery. They import Negro slaves to the West Indies. France, Holland and England reach the New World. Drake raids the Pacific and claims California for England, while the French explore the St Lawrence valley.	

Glossary

agave or maguey type of cactus found in Mexico. The Aztecs used the cactus for cloth, thatching for huts and to make an alcoholic drink.

aqueduct a man-made channel for carrying water, often raised above ground.

astrologer priest who studied the stars and how their movement affected life on earth.

calmecac boarding school where boys were trained to be priests.

chinampa small plot of land reclaimed from the mud of the lake. Plots were used for growing crops.

cochineal red dye produced from crushing thousands of tiny red insects.

codex European name for old Aztec manuscript.

glyphs tiny pictures used for writing instead of words.

incense substance burnt at religious ceremonies to produce exotic fragrances.

jade semi-precious stone, green in colour. The Aztecs considered it very precious and only nobles were allowed to wear it.

obsidian volcanic glass used to make spearheads and blades for clubs.

quetzal a bird of the pheasant family, prized for its feathers, which only the king and high nobles were allowed to wear.

squash vegetable rather like a pumpkin grown by the Aztecs. It was unknown in Europe before the Spanish Conquest.

telpochcalli clan school where boys trained as warriors. They learned the use of war weapons, watched over by a trained warrior or elder.

tortilla flat pancake made from maize and baked on a flat griddle.

tribute goods and wealth paid to the Aztecs by smaller neighbouring tribes.

turquoise semi-precious stone, worn by Aztec nobility. The colour turquoise was sacred and was worn only by the Aztec king to show his high rank.

war of flowers a war arranged between neighbouring tribes allowing each side to take prisoners. These were for sacrifice to the gods.

Index

Numbers in bold refer to illustrations

African history (1100-1500), 59
Agave cactus, **21**
Amaranth, 21
American history (1100-1500), 59
Animals, 17, 18, **18**, **47**
Aqueducts, **20**, 54, 60
Arts and crafts, 38-9, **38-9**
Asian history (1100-1500), 58
Astrology, 22, **30**, **31**, 32-3, **32-3**, 51, 54, 60
Atlatl, **40**

Babies, 22, **22**, **23**, 30
Ball courts, **9**, 28, **28**
Barter, 10, 15, 45, 50, **50**
Bathhouse, **17**
Battles, 41, **42-3**, 43
Beans, 18, 21, **21**
Black body paint, **31**, 37
Blue Hummingbird, **11**, 36, 38, 42, 44, 51, 54, 55
Boats, **11**
Books, 52-3, **52-3**
Boys, 22, **22**, **23**, 24, **28**, **30-1**, **40-1**, **42**

Calendars, 32-3, **33**, 54
Calmecac (priests' school), **9**, **30**, 47, 60
Canals, **10**, 12, **20**, 21, 41
Chapultepec (Grasshopper Hill), **39**, 58
Charles V, King of Spain, **47**
Chichen Itza, **28**
Chiefs, 8, **11**, 12, **13**
Children, 22, **22-3**, 25, 32
Chinampas, 21, 60
Clans, 12, **13**, 21, **23**, 25, **40**, **42**, 44, 52
Cloaks, 12, **12**, 26, **27**, 39, 45, **46**, 47
Cloth, **21**, **25**, 26, 27, 38, **38**
Clothes, 12, **12**, 25, 26-7, **27**, **40**, **42**, **43**, 45, 49, 53
Clubs, **40**, 60
Coatlicue, Mother Earth, 51, **51**
Cochineal, 26, 60
Cocoa, **19**, 54
Cocoa beans, 15, 50, **50**
Codex, 52-3, **53**, 60
Columbus, Christopher, 56
Conch shells, 8
Cooking, 18, **18-19**, 23
Cornelian, **39**

Cortes, Hernan, **47**, 48, **49**, 55, 56, 58
Cotton, **25**, 26, 54
Council of chiefs, 8, 12, 46
Craftsmen, 10, **13**, 17, **23**, 26, 36, 38-9, **38-9**, 47, 54
Crimes and punishments, 12, **12**, 14, **15**, **23**, 41

Dancing and singing, 8, 28, 35, **37**, **39**, **41**
Diaz, Bernal, 6, 14
Digging stick, 17, **21**
Dogs, 15, 18, **18**
Domestic animals, 17, 18, **18**

Eagle warriors, **35**, 36, **41**, **43**, 53, **53**
Ear plug, **26**
Education, 22, **22-3**, **30-1**, **40-1**, 47, 51
Entertainment, **19**, 28, 47
European history (1100-1500), 58
Evening Star, god of the, **32**

Farmers, 6, 12, 21, **21**, **25**, **26**, 27, 51
Feathers, featherworking, 15, **27**, 38, **38**, 40, **43**, 45, **47**, 54, 60
Festival of the Lords, 35
Festivals, 8, **8-9**, 35, **34-5**, 51
Fish, fishing, 10, 17, 18, **18**, **23**
Food, 10, 12, **12**, 18, **18-19**, 21, **21**
Foreign affairs, 12, **13**, 46
Frogs, 10, 18, **25**, 54

Games, 28, **28-9**
Gardens, 17
Girls, 22, **22**, **23**, 24, 26, **26**, **27**, 28
Glyphs, 52-3, **53**, 60
God of Flowers, **39**
God of the Spring Festival, 35
Gods, 8, **11**, **16**, 22, 25, **30**, **31**, 32, **32**, **34-5**, 35, 36, **36-7**, **39**, **40**, 42, 43, 51, **51**, 55
Gold, goldworking, 6, 15, **23**, 36, 38, **38**, 39, **39**, 54, 55
Greasy pole competition, 28

Hair styles, **26**
Headdresses, **27**, 39, **43**, **47**
Healers, 25, **25**
Heaven and hell, 51
Helmets, **43**
Herbal medicines, 15, 25, **25**, **31**
Hernandez, **14**
High Court of Justice, 8
Houses, **16-17**, 17

Illnesses, 25, **25**, 48
Incas, 56
Incense, 36, **37**, 60
Indian turnip, **25**

Jade, 39, 60
Jaguar warriors, **41**, **43**
Jewellery, 12, **12**, 15, **23**, 26, **26**, 36, 39, 45, **47**, 60
Jimson weed, **25**
Juggling, **19**, 28
Juniper, **25**

King, 8, 12, **12**, **13**, 21, 32, 39, 44, 45, 46-7, **46-7**, 60

Lake Texcoco, 6, 10, **10**, **11**, 54, 58
Land, 6, 10, 12, **13**, 21, 25, 52, 54, 60
Laws, 12, **12**, 14, 41, 44, 52
Lip plug, **26**
Lizard, roast, **25**
"Load", 50
Loincloth, 26, 27
Lord and Lady of Death, 51

Magellan, Fernando, 55
Magic, 25, **31**, 48, 55
Maize, 18, **18**, 21, **21**
Markets, 8, 14-15, **14**, 50, 55
Marriage, 24, **24**, **26**
"Master of Cuts", **41**, 47
Matchmaker, 24, **24**, 25
Maya, **28**, 33
Merchants, **13**, 45
Mexico City, **10**, **11**
Midwives, 22, 25, 32
Military commanders, **13**
Mixtec-style warrior, 53, **53**
Montezuma I, King, 54, 58
Montezuma II, King, 18, 46-7, **46-7**, 48, **48**, 55, 58
Mother Earth, 51, **51**
Music, **19**, 28, **39**, 47

Names, **32**
Naming ceremony, 22, **30**, 32
Near Eastern history (1100-1500), 59
New Fire Ceremony, 35
New World exploration, 56
Nobles, 6, **8**, 12, **12**, **13**, 17, **19**, 21, **27**, 28, 45, **46**, 60
Nose plug, **26**

Obsidian, 39, **40**, 43, 49, 60
Officials, 12, **12**, **13**, 14, **23**, 46, **46**
Omens, **48**

Painting and drawing, **22-3**, 32, 52-3, **53**
Palace of Axayacatl, **11**
Palaces, 8, **11**, 15, 17, 47, **47**, **48**
Pancakes, 18, **18**, 60
Paper-making, 52, **52**
Patolli, **28**
Peasants, 12, **13**, **16-17**, 17, 18, 23, **41**
Pizarro, Francisco, 56
Plays, 28
Poetry recitals, **28**
Portuguese, 56
Pottery, 15, **16**, **27**, 50
Prices, 50, **50**
Priests, **8**, **23**, **30-1**, 32, **37**, 47, 52, 60
Prisoners-of-war, **13**, 15, 32
Pulque, **21**
Puppies, roast, 15, **18**

Quails, **30**
Quauhtitlan, 53
Quetzal bird, **30**, 38, **47**, 60
Quetzalcoatl, **11**, **30**, 48, 51, 54, 55

Rabbits, 17, 18
Religious ceremonies, **8**, **31**, **34-5**, 35, 36, 60
Rush mats, 15, **16**, 17

Sacred calendar, 32-3, **33**, 54
Sacrifices, 8, **15**, **30**, **31**, 32, **34-5**, 35, 36, **37**, 43, 51
Sage, 18, 21
Scribes, **30**, 43, **44**, 52, 53
Serpent wall, **9**
Shields, 38, **38**, **40**
Skull rack, **9**, 49
Slaves, **13**, 15, **15**, 21, **23**, **50**
Sleeping mats, **16**, 17
Snake Woman, 8, 12, **13**, 46
Solar calendar, 33, **33**, 54
Soothsayers, **30**, 48
Spaniards, 6, 14, **16**, **21**, 36, **36**, 39, 48-9, **49**, 53, **55**, 55, 56, 58
Spears, **40**, 49, 60
Squash, 21, **21**
Stars, watching the, **31**, 32-3, **32-3**, 54
Sun god, worship of, **31**, 35, 51, **51**

Tadpoles, 18
Taxation, 12, 44
Teacher, **23**
Telpochcalli, **40**
Temple of Quetzalcoatl, **9**
Temple of Tezcatlipoca, **9**
Temple of the Sun, **9**
Temple platform, 8, **9**, 36, **37**, **55**
Temples and shrines, **9**, **31**, 36, **36-7**, **41**, 51, 52, 54
Tenayuca temple, 36
Tenochca tribe (Aztecs), 10
Tenochtitlan, 6, 8, **8-9**, 10, **11**, **20**, 36, **36-7**, 43, 44, **53**, 54, **54**, 55, 58
Tepanec tribe, 10, 58
Texcoco, 54, 55
Thieves, **12**, 14, **15**, **23**
Tlachtli, 28, **29**
Tlacopan, 54
Tlaloc, god of rain, 36, 51, 54, 55
Tlatelolco market, 14, 55
Tobacco-smoking, **19**
Toltecs, 10, 39, 47, 51, 54, 58
Tomatoes, 18, 21, **21**
Tonatiuh, sun god, **51**
Tortillas, 15, 18, **18**, **30**, 60
Trade, **13**, 14-15, **14-15**, 42, 45, 51
Tribute, **8**, 10, 43, 44, **44**, 46, 52, 54, 60
Turkeys, 17, 18
Turquoise, **12**, 60

Valley of Mexico, 6, 10, **11**, 36, 51, 54, 56, 58
Vegetables, 15, 21, **21**
Vera Cruz, 48, 58
Volador Ceremony, **35**

War and conquest, 12, **13**, 32, 42-3, **42-3**, 44, **44**, 47, 48-9, 54, **54**, 55, **55**
War of Flowers, 43
Warriors, **8**, 12, **13**, 22, **26**, **28**, 39, **40-1**, **42-3**, 44, 46, 47, **48**, 51, 53, **53**, **54**
Weapons, 35, **40**, 43, 49, 60
Weaving, **23**, 25, **25**, 27
Weights and measures, 50
Wives, 25, **25**
Women, **8**, 16, 17, 18, **18**, 24-5, **25**, **26**, 27, 35, 51
Woodcarving, **23**
Writing and reading, **31**, 51, 52-3, **53**